GRAINS

Healthy Plates

VALERIE BODDEN

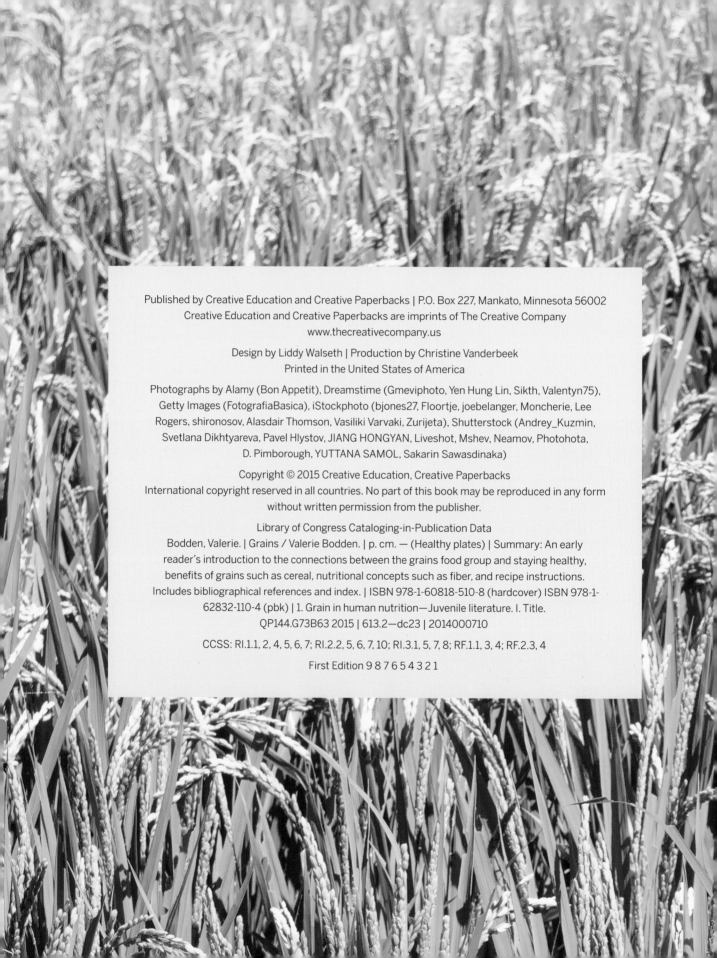

Published by Creative Education and Creative Paperbacks | P.O. Box 227, Mankato, Minnesota 56002
Creative Education and Creative Paperbacks are imprints of The Creative Company
www.thecreativecompany.us

Design by Liddy Walseth | Production by Christine Vanderbeek
Printed in the United States of America

Photographs by Alamy (Bon Appetit), Dreamstime (Gmeviphoto, Yen Hung Lin, Sikth, Valentyn75),
Getty Images (FotografiaBasica), iStockphoto (bjones27, Floortje, joebelanger, Moncherie, Lee
Rogers, shironosov, Alasdair Thomson, Vasiliki Varvaki, Zurijeta), Shutterstock (Andrey_Kuzmin,
Svetlana Dikhtyareva, Pavel Hlystov, JIANG HONGYAN, Liveshot, Mshev, Neamov, Photohota,
D. Pimborough, YUTTANA SAMOL, Sakarin Sawasdinaka)

Library of Congress Cataloging-in-Publication Data
Bodden, Valerie. | Grains / Valerie Bodden. | p. cm. — (Healthy plates) | Summary: An early
reader's introduction to the connections between the grains food group and staying healthy,
benefits of grains such as cereal, nutritional concepts such as fiber, and recipe instructions.
Includes bibliographical references and index. | ISBN 978-1-60818-510-8 (hardcover) ISBN 978-1-
62832-110-4 (pbk) | 1. Grain in human nutrition—Juvenile literature. I. Title.
QP144.G73B63 2015 | 613.2—dc23 | 2014000710

CCSS: RI.1.1, 2, 4, 5, 6, 7; RI.2.2, 5, 6, 7, 10; RI.3.1, 5, 7, 8; RF.1.1, 3, 4; RF.2.3, 4

First Edition 9 8 7 6 5 4 3 2 1

TABLE OF CONTENTS

GRAINS AND VEGETABLES
LIKE POTATOES HAVE A
NUTRIENT CALLED STARCH.

Growing Up

Your body needs food to give it energy and help it grow. But not all foods are good for you. Healthy foods contain the **nutrients** (*NOO-tree-unts*) your body needs to be at its best. Healthy foods are put into five food groups: dairy, fruits, grains, **proteins**, and vegetables. Your body needs foods from each food group every day.

Grain Group

Grains are the seeds of grasses such as wheat, rice, oats, and barley. Bread, pasta, and cereal are made from grains. Grains have nutrients called carbohydrates (*kar-bo-HI-drates*). Carbohydrates give your body energy.

THE CEREAL GRAINS PICTURED ARE RYE, WHEAT, OAT, AND PEARL BARLEY.

Whole and Refined

Some grains are called "whole grains." This means that they use the whole grain seed. Brown rice, oatmeal, and popcorn are whole grains. Most whole grains have a lot of fiber. Fiber is good for your **digestive system**.

THREE CUPS OF AIR-POPPED POPCORN CONTAIN 3.5 GRAMS OF FIBER.

Whole grains have many **vitamins**. The B vitamins in whole grains help keep your heart and brain healthy. They help your body use energy from food.

GRANOLA BARS ARE
OFTEN MADE WITH WHOLE
GRAINS LIKE OATS.

Other grains are called "re-fined grains." White bread and white rice are refined grains. Parts of the grain seed are taken off refined grains. This makes them last longer. But removing the seed takes out fiber and nutrients.

WHITE RICE IS BROWN RICE WITHOUT THE HULL, OR OUTER SHELL.

Sometimes nutrients are put back into refined grains. B vitamins are added to many refined grains. So is iron. Iron helps your blood carry **oxygen**.

LIGHTER-COLORED SPAGHETTI NOODLES ARE MADE FROM REFINED GRAINS.

How Much?

Most kids should get three to five ounces (85–142 g) of grains a day. At least half the grains should be whole grains. A slice of bread or

one cup (237 ml) of cereal counts as one ounce of grains. People who are older or more active can eat more grains.

Healthy Living

It is easy to eat more whole grains. Try some oatmeal for breakfast. Make a sandwich on whole-grain bread for lunch. Grab some popcorn for a snack.

Eating grains is part of being healthy. Exercising is another part. Try to move your body an hour every day. Exercising and eating healthy can be fun—and can make you feel good, too!

PLAY TAG WITH A FRIEND OR DO GYMNASTICS TO MAKE EXERCISE FUN!

MAKE A GRAIN SNACK:

POPCORN SNACK MIX

1 BAG PLAIN MICROWAVE POPCORN
2 CUPS WHOLE-GRAIN PRETZELS
1 CUP WHOLE-GRAIN CEREAL
1 CUP DRIED FRUIT SUCH AS RAISINS
2 TBSP. GRATED PARMESAN CHEESE

Pop the popcorn, and empty it into a bowl. Add the pretzels, cereal, and raisins. Mix and top with Parmesan. Enjoy your healthy whole-grain snack!

GLOSSARY

digestive system—the parts of your body used in breaking down food and getting rid of waste

nutrients—the parts of food that your body uses to make energy, grow, and stay healthy

oxygen—a gas, or type of air, that people need to breathe

proteins—foods such as meat and nuts that contain the nutrient protein, which helps the body grow

vitamins—nutrients found in foods that are needed to keep your body healthy and working well

READ MORE

Head, Honor. *Healthy Eating*. Mankato, Minn.: Sea-to-Sea, 2013.

Kalz, Jill. *Grains*. North Mankato, Minn.: Smart Apple Media, 2004.

Llewellyn, Claire. *Healthy Eating*. Laguna Hills, Calif.: QEB, 2006.

WEBSITES

My Plate Kids' Place
http://www.choosemyplate.gov/kids/index.html
Check out games, activities, and recipes about eating healthy.

PBS Kids: Healthy Eating Games
http://pbskids.org/games/healthyeating.html
Play games that help you learn about healthy foods.

Note: Every effort has been made to ensure that the websites listed above are suitable for children, that they have educational value, and that they contain no inappropriate material. However, because of the nature of the Internet, it is impossible to guarantee that these sites will remain active indefinitely or that their contents will not be altered.

INDEX